Polar Bears

NATURE'S PREDATORS

Eleanor J. Hall

KidHaven Press

KidHaven Press, an imprint of Gale Group, Inc.
P.O. Box 289009, San Diego, CA 92198-9009

Library of Congress Cataloging-in-Publication Data

Hall, Eleanor J.
    Polar Bears / by Eleanor J. Hall.
       p. cm. — (Nature's predators)
    Includes bibliographical references.
    Summary: Discusses the physical characteristics of polar bears,
    their hunting style, physical characteristics, eating and sleeping
    habits, their natural enemies, and their use by zoos.
    ISBN 0-7377-0701-1 (hardcover : alk. paper)
    1. Polar bear—Juvenile literature. [1. Polar bear. 2. Bears.] I.
    Title. II. Series.
    QL737.C27 H358 2002
    599.786—dc21

                                              2001002249

Contents

Chapter 1

Earth's Largest Land Predators

The bears that live in the cold Arctic region of the earth are known by many names. Americans call them polar bears, but in many other countries they are known as ice bears. The Inuit people (Eskimos) have given them names that mean "the white bear," "the ghost bear," or "the ever-wandering one." To scientists, who use Latin names to classify animals, polar bears are called *Ursus maritimus,* meaning "bear of the sea."

As fitting as these names are, none of them fully describes the awesome size and strength of polar bears, the largest land **predators** on Earth. The average weight of a full-grown male polar bear is around one thousand pounds, or half a ton. A few may weigh as much as fifteen hundred pounds. When standing on their hind feet, as they often do, some male polar bears rise to ten feet tall. Female polar bears are about half the size and weight of males. "No predator on earth approaches him in size," writes **naturalist** Richard C. Davids. "Polar bears are twice as big as lions and tigers. . . . His paws are a foot wide. When he stands erect, he can look an elephant in the eye."[1]

Size and strength are very important to polar bears because the seals and walruses they hunt for food are also large and strong. Seals weigh from two hundred to four hundred pounds. Walruses weigh much more and have long, sharp tusks to defend themselves. However, as important as size and strength are, polar bears must rely on many other physical traits and skills to survive in their frigid homeland.

Physical Traits

The Arctic polar region is the only place on Earth where polar bears live in the wild. In the areas closest to the North Pole, both land and sea are covered with a thick layer of ice and snow year-round. There are no trees or other large plants for polar bears to hide behind while hunting.

Farther south in the Arctic, the ground is covered with low-growing plants called **tundra.** For most of the year, the tundra is covered under a deep blanket of snow. Even in the short summer season (which lasts about six weeks), tundra never grows tall enough to conceal a polar bear.

Since there are few places for polar bears to hide from their **prey,** nature has provided them

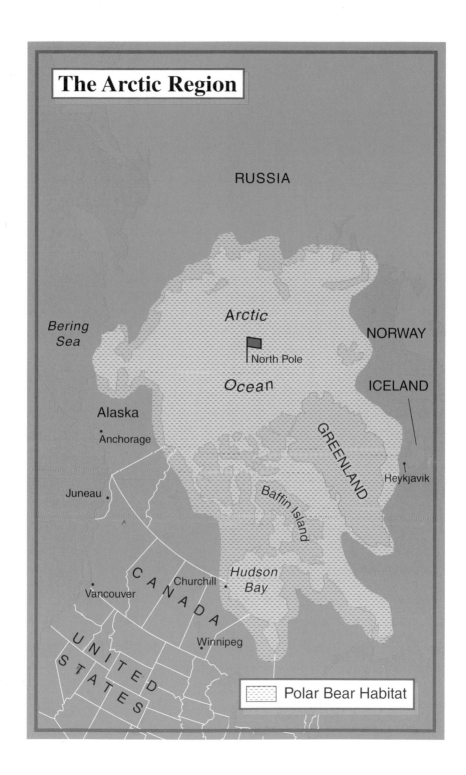

The Arctic Region

RUSSIA

Bering
Sea

Arctic

North Pole

NORWAY

ICELAND

Ocean

Alaska

GREENLAND

Anchorage

Reykjavik

Juneau

Baffin Island

CANADA

Churchill

Hudson
Bay

Vancouver

UNITED

Winnipeg

STATES

Polar Bear Habitat

with white (or nearly white) fur to blend in with the snowy landscape. That is why the Inuit call them "ghost bears"—they seem to appear out of nowhere. Although light-colored fur is valuable for sneaking up on seals and other prey, it also has another important use: White fur helps keep polar bears warm.

For a long time, scientists did not understand how this could be. Light colors cool the body by reflecting the sun's rays while dark colors soak up the heat. The mystery was finally solved when scientists looked at polar bear fur under a powerful microscope. They discovered that the guard hairs, or outer coat, of a polar bear's fur are hollow. Rays from the sun travel through these tiny tubes to the bear's skin. The skin, which is black, traps the heat inside the bear's body. Just beneath the skin, there is a four- to five-inch layer of fat, called **blubber,** that also helps keep out the cold.

Polar bears are further protected from cold temperatures by their streamlined bodies. They have long noses, small heads, and slender necks that allow cold winds to flow around them. They also have short tails and small ears, so there is less body surface from which heat can escape.

In contrast to their slender upper bodies, polar bears have short, stocky legs and enormous paws to provide the strength and endurance needed in hunting. A polar bear's large paws serve the same purpose as snowshoes do for people. They spread out the bear's weight so it doesn't sink into the

A polar bear's large paws are like snowshoes for people. They keep the bear from slipping on ice or sinking into snow.

snow when walking or running. The soles of its feet are covered with tough, bumpy skin to prevent the bear from slipping on the ice.

All of these characteristics help polar bears hunt successfully. However, the physical features that make polar bears one of the world's most dangerous predators are their huge claws and sharp teeth. Each paw is equipped with five claws that are about two inches long and are very thick. They use them to capture and kill their prey.

Claws are useful in many other ways, too. Polar bears dig their claws into the ice to run faster and to keep from falling on slick surfaces. Bears also use their claws for digging their own dens or for breaking into the dens of other animals.

In addition to their claws, polar bears have forty-two teeth of several different types: **canine teeth** to kill prey, **incisors** to rip and tear the tough hides of seals, and **molars** to chew and grind the meat. With natural weapons such as these, it does not take long for a polar bear to kill and eat a large seal.

Senses: Sight, Hearing, Smell

Polar bears also rely on sight, hearing, and smell to catch their prey. According to studies by naturalists, polar bears can see and hear as well as humans. Their sense of smell is far greater than that of humans, however. According to Norbert Rosing, a naturalist who has studied the habits of polar bears for many years, a polar bear can smell a seal hidden under six feet of snow from a quarter of a mile away.

Polar bears rely heavily on their sense of smell all year. It is especially valuable during the winter, however, when darkness and fierce blizzards make it hard to see or hear.

Getting Around

The polar bear's legs and paws are also well suited to the Arctic landscape. Polar bears seem a bit awkward when they walk. The big paws on their front legs turn in slightly as they move, giv-

Scientists have named the polar bear "the bear of the sea" because the animal is a good swimmer and can tolerate the cold water.

---

ing them a pigeon-toed appearance. They also swing their heads slowly back and forth as they lumber along.

When it comes to running, though, polar bears are anything but awkward. Even the biggest bears can move swiftly. Young males are the fastest runners. Some have been clocked at thirty-five miles an hour over short distances. They are amazing jumpers, too. When hunting on the sea ice, they often jump from one ice floe, or sheet of floating ice, to another.

When the distances are too great to jump across, polar bears dive into the sea and swim. Their nostrils close up when they dive, and they can stay underwater for two minutes. No one knows exactly how deeply they dive, but they probably go no deeper than twenty feet. They use their front legs and paws to move forward and their back legs to guide them through the water.

Polar bears have great endurance in the water and have been known to swim as far as one hundred miles at one time. Their swimming speed is about six miles an hour. Staying in the frigid water for a long time does not bother them. The blubber inside their bodies keeps them warm, and their fur easily sheds water.

In fact, polar bears often become overheated when hunting or playing. When this happens, they take a dip in the sea to cool off. When they get out, they shake energetically and roll in the snow to dry.

All of these natural features and skills help polar bears hunt and kill their prey. Even with their many abilities, though, hunting is never easy. Seals and other animals hunted by polar bears have developed their own skills to keep from being eaten. As a result, the struggle between polar bears and their prey never ends.

Chapter 2

How Polar Bears Hunt

In the high Arctic, near the North Pole, the ice and snow never melts. For the few polar bears that live in this region, hunting does not change very much from winter to summer. Farther south, much of the ice and snow melts during the short summer season. Seals are more difficult to catch when the ice melts, so bears must hunt smaller kinds of prey.

Wherever they live, polar bears hunt alone. They do not form packs or help each other kill prey. The only exception is a mother bear with cubs. Cubs stay with their mothers for two to three years. Even in those cases, however, the mother bear does the killing while the cubs watch and learn how to do it themselves.

Seal Hunting

Seals are the favorite food of polar bears. Several different kinds of seals live in the Arctic, but polar bears catch ringed seals most often. Their name comes from ring-shaped designs on their skin. Even though ringed seals are the smallest of the seal family, adults weigh about two hundred pounds. Most of this weight is in the form of blubber, a welcome treat for polar bears. Bears also hunt bearded seals, which are quite a bit larger than ringed seals. An adult bearded seal may weigh four to five hundred pounds.

Seal hunting is best before the winter ice begins to thaw. As the ice melts during the short summer, seals move farther out to sea. To catch them, bears are forced to swim across large ex-

Except for a mother bear that has cubs, polar bears hunt alone.

panses of water. Although bears are good swimmers, seals are so much better and faster that bears rarely catch them in the sea. To hunt seals successfully, bears must go to the ice.

Although seals spend most of their time underneath water or ice, they must come to the surface to breathe every twenty minutes or so. When the sea freezes in winter, seals cut breathing holes in the ice with sharp claws that grow on their front flippers. As the ice gets thicker, they keep the holes open by constantly scraping the new ice away.

Seals also make larger holes so they can pull themselves out onto the ice to rest or, in the case of females, to have babies.

With its keen sense of smell, a polar bear quickly locates a seal's den hidden under layers of snow. The bear walks up to it quietly and then suddenly pounces on it to break through the snow. If a seal pup is inside the den, the bear grabs it with its huge paws and eats it in one or two gulps.

Catching older seals is not so easy. A polar bear knows that a swimming seal must come to the surface often, so it sniffs out a breathing hole in the ice and waits. Seals have a few tricks of their own, however. They may carve out as many as ten or twelve breathing holes. If a seal suspects a bear is waiting at one hole, it goes to another to get air. Nevertheless, a polar bear is patient when hunting. It may wait silently by a breathing hole for hours, knowing the slightest noise will frighten the seal away.

A polar bear pounces into the snow after smelling a seal.

Polar bears use another method to catch seals that are resting on the ice. Resting seals sit up often to watch for predators, so a hunting bear must sneak up quietly. If there happen to be snowdrifts or ridges of ice to hide behind, the bear slips up as close as possible without being seen. If there is nothing to hide behind, the bear lies on its stomach and pushes itself forward with its back feet. If the seal looks up, the bear freezes in place. At the last moment, it leaps up and attacks. Sometimes bears catch resting seals by swimming toward them underwater. When they reach the ice shelf where the seal is lying, they suddenly spring out of the water and take the seal by surprise. It is extremely hard to catch a seal by surprise, however. More often than not, the seal sees or hears the bear before it gets too close and quickly escapes into the sea.

Hunting Walruses and Other Large Animals

Walruses are another kind of sea animal hunted by polar bears. Walruses gather by the hundreds on Arctic beaches and **ice floes.** Hunting walruses is much more difficult and dangerous for polar bears than hunting seals. Some walruses weigh as much as three thousand pounds and have long, sharp tusks to defend themselves.

For many years, it was unclear whether polar bears actually hunted and killed walruses or whether they just ate dead ones that washed up on beaches. The mystery was solved in 1990 when

Seals give birth under the snow, making them and their pups easy targets for a hungry bear.

naturalist Nikita Ovsyanikov studied polar bears on Wrangel Island in the Arctic Ocean.

Ovsyanikov observed and filmed two walrus hunts. The first was a mother bear that dove into a group of adult walruses and snatched a calf. When a large male bear suddenly appeared and took her catch away from her, she went back and caught another calf the same way.

Ovsyanikov also filmed a large male bear trying to kill an adult walrus. When walruses rest on the shore, they huddle closely together for warmth and protection. When attacked, they head for the sea as fast as they can. When the bear being filmed suddenly pounced on a group of walruses, they scattered into the water—all but one old female. She was too old and tired to reach the water quickly. When the bear got close to her, she lunged at it with her sharp tusks, over and over again. To avoid being cut by her tusks, the bear got behind her and jumped on her back. Still fighting, the old walrus struggled toward the sea and finally escaped into the water.

Attacking an adult walrus is clearly dangerous for a bear. But bears that are really hungry—as this one was—will take great risks. In a few cases, polar bears have killed such large animals as caribou, musk oxen, and small whales that got trapped in low water. When seals and other large prey are unavailable, though, polar bears are forced to go after small animals, which barely make a bite for their powerful jaws.

Hunting Small Animals

Most polar bears live where seals are scarce in summer. In these areas, they hunt smaller prey such as rabbits, ground squirrels, ducks, and lemmings. Lemmings are small rodents weighing only a few ounces—barely a taste for a polar bear. At certain times of year, thousands of these small creatures run around on the tundra. According to naturalist Richard C. Davids, it is a comical sight "to watch an 800-pound bear stalking a two-ounce lemming.... Still, the bears hunt lemmings

A really hungry polar bear will eat anything, even small animals such as rabbits and squirrels.

with great glee, making short rushes in the grass and pouncing, although the lemmings usually evade [escape] them."[2]

People as Prey

Although many people have been killed by polar bears, there is disagreement on whether bears actually hunt people for food, as they would hunt

Polar bears seem curious about people and will often come right up to vehicle windows to get a good look.

seals or walruses. In most of the cases in which bears have stalked people or broken into cabins after them, the bears were extremely hungry.

Ovsyanikov and many other naturalists believe that polar bears are more curious about people than they are aggressive toward them. Bears often press their noses against cabin windows to see what the strangers inside are doing. Outside the cabin, anything unusual attracts their attention. They climb on vehicles and on the roofs of buildings. They examine objects with their long noses and big paws. Because they are so large and strong, their curiosity often makes them destructive.

When Ovsyanikov studied polar bears on Wrangel Island, he never carried a gun. Instead, he watched bears closely to learn how they behaved toward each other. He then imitated their actions when he was among them. In eight seasons of work, he was never harmed by a bear.

Nevertheless, neither Ovsyanikov nor anyone else doubts that polar bears are dangerous predators. Even a friendly bear may turn aggressive if suddenly frightened by an unexpected sound or movement. For the most part, though, polar bears concentrate on hunting seals, not people.

Like all predators, polar bears never know when, or from where, their next meal is coming. They may be feasting on fat seals one week and fasting (going without any food) the next week. Nevertheless, nature has provided them with ways to survive, even when food is scarce.

Chapter 3

Feasting and Fasting

Animals as large as polar bears need a lot of food to survive; they especially need the fat, or blubber, that comes from seals and walruses. Exactly how many seals are eaten by polar bears each year is unknown. However, naturalists believe that adult polar bears need about four and a half pounds of fat per day to stay healthy.

Of course, polar bears do not eat every day. They may not be able to catch anything, or they may not be hungry. Polar bears can go for days without eating after devouring a large seal. When they stuff themselves, as they often do, any extra fat is stored in their bodies to tide them over between kills.

The Importance of Blubber

Eating blubber and storing the fat from it is necessary for all polar bears. For females who are going to have cubs, it is especially important. A mother-to-be spends the summer months eating as much as she can. In the fall, she digs a den beneath deep snowdrifts and shuts herself and her cubs inside.

Mother and cubs stay in the den for seven or eight months while the cubs grow stronger. During this time, the mother lives off of the fat from the seal blubber she ate during the summer. She feeds her cubs with rich milk from her body. When they come out of the den in the spring, each cub has a thick coat of white fur and weighs over twenty pounds. Unlike her cubs, the mother bear is quite thin and is extremely hungry by this time. It has been months since she has eaten. As soon as her cubs are able to travel beside her safely, she heads for the seashore to catch a seal.

Although polar bears depend on seal and walrus blubber for survival, they will eat just about anything when they are hungry. This includes berries and certain other plants that grow during the short summer. They also eat kelp, a nourishing kind of seaweed. Being able to hunt on both land and sea gives polar bears a wide range of food choices. In addition, they are **scavengers** as well as predators.

Polar Bears as Scavengers

Scavengers are animals that eat prey that has been killed by another animal or that has died from other causes. Walruses and seals that die in the sea eventually wash up on beaches. Polar bears sniff out their **carcasses** and feast on them for days.

In 1999 forty beluga whales got trapped by ice in a shallow bay in northern Canada. Beluga whales are small compared to many other whales, but they have sharp teeth and are bigger than polar bears. Ordinarily, it would be impossible for a polar bear to kill a beluga whale; however, these whales were in shallow water and were unable to get away. Polar bears for miles around caught their scent and rushed to the scene.

Naturalist Malcolm Ramsay flew over the site in a helicopter. He counted twenty-five bears there

A polar bear feasts on a beluga whale. Bears prefer the blubber of the whale and will often leave the meat behind.

Hungry polar bears will even scavenge for and eat human garbage.

at one time, feasting on the trapped whales. Ramsay landed and **tranquilized** one male bear and two females in order to weigh them. (Tranquilizing puts them to sleep for a short time, but it does not harm them.) "The male weighed 1,037 pounds—one of the biggest I've ever handled," Ramsay reports, "and the females were almost twice as heavy as they normally are in the spring. The bears had put on so much weight that they could go without feeding for almost a year."[3]

Killing, Sharing, and Eating Prey

When not scavenging, a polar bear uses its claws and teeth in one swift motion to kill large prey, such as a seal. First it stuns the seal with its front paws and claws. Then it bites it through the head and neck several times. In less time than it takes to tell about it, the bear drags the seal onto the ice and begins eating it.

Polar bears usually eat alone, but at certain times they will share food. Mother bears always share food with their cubs. Adult bears sometimes eat together for practical reasons, such as helping each other tear open the tough hide of a big seal or walrus.

Another instance of sharing is when a strong bear allows a less powerful bear to eat some of its food. This kind of sharing follows strict body language rules. First, the bear that is asking for food

A mother bear shares a meal of seal with her cubs.

walks in a wide circle around the bear with the food. As it walks, it moves its head slowly up and down. This signifies that it only wants food and means no harm. With each circle, it gets closer and closer. Finally, the two bears meet and touch noses. Then, and only then, will the lesser bear be allowed to eat.

Although sharing does happen, stealing food is probably more common. Bears are always in a hurry to eat because a more powerful bear may suddenly show up and drive them away from their dinner. Occasionally, a mother bear will risk her life to chase a male bear away from a kill she has made. Most of the time, lesser bears simply keep out of the way until the biggest bears have eaten their fill.

When bears eat, they do not chew their food thoroughly; instead, they swallow it in big chunks. First they eat the skin and blubber, then the meat. If a bear is not particularly hungry, it may eat only the blubber. If it is extremely hungry, only the bones will be left behind.

Polar bears are neat animals. They do not like to be dirty or messy. After eating, they always clean their blood-stained fur in the sea. Some bears are so tidy that they stop and wash their paws and faces even before they finish a meal.

Staying Alive

Getting enough to eat is a constant problem for all polar bears, but it is even harder for some. Very old bears that can no longer hunt effectively often starve to death. Young bears on their own have a hard time, too. When a mother bear decides her cubs are old enough to hunt for themselves, she simply walks off and leaves them while they are sleeping. Because their hunting skills are not well developed, some of them do not survive.

It is possible for wild polar bears to live as long as thirty years, but most only survive about fifteen to eighteen years. The oldest wild bear that natu-

Dr. Malcolm Ramsay extracts a tooth from the mouth of a sedated adult polar bear to determine the bear's age.

ralists have discovered was thirty-two years old when it died. In zoos, where they eat regularly, bears may sometimes live longer.

An Unusual Predator Relationship

When hunting and eating, polar bears have an unusual relationship with a small animal—the Arctic fox. Like polar bears, Arctic foxes do not sleep through the winter. Although their white fur coats keep them from freezing, they have a hard time finding food during the long winter. The lemmings, rabbits, and birds they usually eat have gone away for the winter or lie sleeping in their winter dens.

In order to survive, Arctic foxes follow polar bears around, waiting for them to make a kill. When that happens, the fox waits nervously until the bear finishes eating. After the bear moves on, the fox rushes in and grabs the leftovers. When bears are hungry, however, they leave little behind for the foxes.

Bears sometimes get irritated with foxes. Occasionally, a bear will charge a fox and try to catch it. They are hardly ever successful, though, because foxes are small and quick. They are also smart enough to keep their distance from an animal many times larger than themselves.

Foxes, as well as all other animals in the Arctic, fear polar bears. For a long time, these giant predators had no match. But when human beings came into their world, everything changed.

Chapter 4

Polar Bear Enemies

Although polar bear cubs are sometimes killed by predators (such as wolves), adult bears are not preyed upon by any other animals. On rare occasions, a walrus may kill an adult polar bear in self-defense, but walruses do not hunt polar bears for food.

Sometimes polar bears are their own worst enemies. Hungry male polar bears will kill and eat unprotected cubs, and even mother bears will eat cubs to keep from starving. At mating time in the spring, male polar bears sometimes injure or kill one another in fights. For the most part, however, polar bears have only one real enemy—people with weapons. Before laws were passed to protect them, polar bears were in great danger of being wiped out by human hunters.

Polar Bears and Native Peoples of the Arctic

Even though Inuit hunters killed polar bears for meat and fur, they also considered them to be

An adult male polar bear eats a polar bear cub.

sacred animals. Out of respect for them, hunters were very careful not to offend a bear's spirit before or after killing it. Some Inuit groups believed the spirit of the dead bear lived for several days in the household of the hunter who killed it. Ceremonies were held to honor the bear spirit, and gifts were given to it.

If any member of the family offended the spirit, the hunter would have no luck on future hunts. However, if proper honor was given, the Inuit believed the bear spirit would take the gifts it received back to the bear world. Living bears would see the gifts and allow themselves to be killed to get gifts of their own. Partly because of these beliefs, and partly because hunters had only stone and bone weapons, the Inuit and polar bears lived in balance for hundreds of years.

The Arrival of Explorers

People who lived far from the Arctic were introduced to polar bears many centuries ago by traders.

Polar bears have only one real enemy—humans.

Cubs were occasionally captured by sailors and were sold as pets in countries outside of the Arctic. These unusual bears were great favorites in the royal courts of Europe, where they were well fed and well treated. Ancient writings reveal that a Japanese emperor, and even an Egyptian pharaoh, owned pet polar bears.

Only the very rich could afford to keep live bears, but less wealthy people could buy their furs. As a result, hunters began killing polar bears and selling their furs for rugs, blankets, and clothing. Even then, however, the polar bear population did not drop very much. Getting the furs to market was slow and difficult, and fur prices were high.

As sailing ships became larger and safer, explorers and traders began to journey into the Arctic in greater numbers. Guns had been invented by this time, and bears were shot from long distances or from the safety of a ship. Inuit hunters soon began using guns also, and the polar bear population dropped rapidly.

Later, after airplanes were invented, the situation became even worse. Hunters were able to travel far up into the Arctic in a short time, and sport hunting became popular in the region. Bears were killed for **trophies** (prizes) to take back home, such as rugs or heads to mount on walls. Hunters often shot bears with high-powered rifles from airplanes and helicopters. On the ground, bears were run down with snowmobiles.

Laws to Protect Bears

People who wanted to save polar bears began protesting to government officials. In 1955 laws were passed in Russia making polar bear hunting illegal. A few years later protection laws were passed in other countries in which polar bears live, including Norway, Canada, the United States, and Greenland (which is governed by Denmark). Not all of these countries banned polar bear hunting completely, but each set strict limits on it.

In 1973 all five countries agreed to work together to protect polar bears. Officials from each country signed the treaty known as International Agreement on Polar Bear **Conservation.** Since that time, many good things have happened for polar bears. Parks have been set aside where bears may live in safety, and naturalists are studying new ways to preserve and protect them.

As a result, polar bear numbers have increased. Naturalists estimate that at least twenty-five thousand—and maybe as many as forty thousand—polar bears exist in the wild today. The exact number cannot be known for sure because the bears are spread out over thousands of square miles.

Even though laws protect polar bears, not everyone obeys them. Illegal hunting, called **poaching,** has become a serious problem in many places. Because the Arctic is so vast and polar bears are so widely scattered, game wardens (officers who track down poachers) have trouble catch-

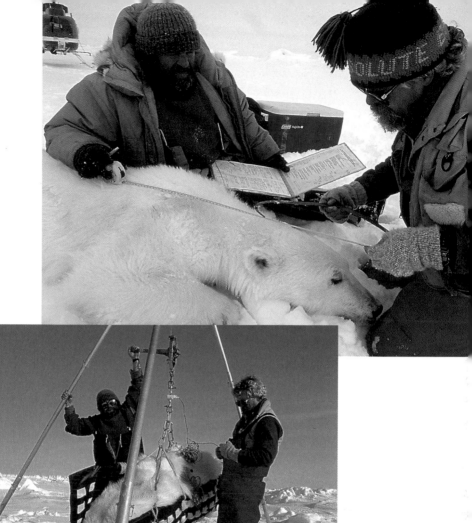

Dr. Malcolm Ramsay and a colleague measure and weigh a tranquilized polar bear. Studying bears will help naturalists and researchers find new ways to help them.

ing poachers. Nevertheless, the new hunting laws have made the future of polar bears a lot brighter.

Other Dangers from People

Outside of a zoo, most people will never see a polar bear, much less hunt one. Nevertheless, even those who have no direct contact with polar bears still have an effect on them. This is because pollution caused by humans is spreading into the Arctic.

Naturalist Malcolm Ramsay has been studying the health of polar bears for many years. Each year he finds higher and higher levels of harmful chemicals in their bodies. Most of the chemicals come from places far from the Arctic. They first enter streams and rivers from factories, garbage dumps, and sewers. From there, they make their way to the ocean, where they enter the bodies of seals. When polar bears eat seals, the chemicals are passed on to them. Another threat to polar bears comes from oil, mining, and other industries moving into the Arctic. No matter how careful such companies may be, accidents sometimes happen that cause great harm to wildlife.

People Working for Polar Bears

Although people cause many problems for polar bears, it is also people who are trying to save them. Working alongside naturalists are those who help get laws passed, educators who teach

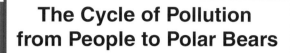

The Cycle of Pollution from People to Polar Bears

Polar Bears eat the contaminated seals and the harmful chemicals pass into their bodies.

People build factories and mine for oil.

Seals eat the contaminated fish.

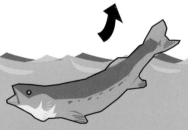

Chemicals from the factories and oil platforms pollute the ocean.

Fish living in the ocean are exposed to the harmful chemicals.

the public about polar bears, and citizens who are interested in saving wild animals.

In recent years naturalists have learned many interesting details about the lives of polar bears. Probably the most surprising is that these mighty predators are more gentle and playful than anyone ever would have guessed. Cubs wrestle in the snow and swim together in the sea. They slide down icy slopes just like children. Young male bears, and even older ones, take part in wrestling matches and make-believe fights in which they are careful not to hurt one another.

The Bears of Churchill, Canada

Many people today have taken such an interest in polar bears that they travel long distances to see and photograph them. Each fall, for example, thousands of tourists travel to Churchill, a small town on Hudson Bay in Canada. In the late fall, hundreds of polar bears gather near Churchill to wait for the bay to freeze. For many years the bears caused numerous problems for the townspeople. Hungry bears were everywhere. They roamed through the town and gathered at the dump grounds to eat garbage.

However, when large numbers of tourists began traveling to Churchill to see the bears, the citizens decided to make the most of it. Hotels, restaurants, and tour services are now available in this small town of about one thousand people. Guides conduct polar bear tours in large vehicles

A polar bear and tourists in tundra buggies observe each other near Churchill, Canada.

called tundra buggies. From the safety of the buggies, tourists and others may quietly watch and photograph polar bears without putting themselves in danger or hurting the bears. Besides tourists, many scientists, photographers, artists, and writers come to Churchill each year.

For the safety of visitors (as well as Churchill's citizens), bears are no longer allowed to roam freely around town. Those bears who wander into town are captured by the "bear police" and are put in a "polar bear jail." When the ice freezes, the bears are moved many miles out of town and are released unharmed. The people of Churchill are now proud to call their town "the Polar Bear Capital of the World."

Polar bears are doing much better today. Hunting laws have allowed their numbers to increase. Naturalists and other scientists are working to improve their health and well-being. Most importantly, more and more people all over the world are becoming interested in saving polar bears and other wild predators from **extinction.**

Notes

1. Richard C. Davids, *Lords of the Arctic: A Journey Among the Polar Bears.* New York: Macmillan, 1982, p. 1.
2. Davids, *Lords of the Arctic,* pp. 41–42.
3. Quoted in *National Geographic,* "Arctic Ice Traps Whales —and Bears Feast," January 2000, p. 21.

Glossary

blubber: A layer of fat inside the bodies of seals, walruses, and polar bears that keeps them from freezing in icy waters. Blubber from seals is the favorite food of polar bears. The fat from the blubber is stored in their bodies to keep them from starving when hunting is bad.

canine teeth: Long, pointed teeth growing on each side of the incisors (front teeth) of polar bears and many other predators. They are used in killing and tearing the tough hides of prey.

carcass: The body of a dead animal.

conservation: Wise and careful use of the earth's resources. One of its goals is preventing animals and plants from becoming endangered or extinct.

extinct: A word referring to living things that once inhabited the earth but no longer exist.

ice floes: Flat chunks of ice that break off larger pieces of ice and float through the sea. Bears sometimes ride on ice floes when they are hunting.

incisors: The front teeth of predators located between the canine teeth. Incisors are useful in cutting and tearing prey.

molars: Large, jagged jaw teeth of predators, used mainly for grinding and chewing food.

naturalist: A scientist who studies plants, animals, birds, and other aspects of nature. Naturalists usually specialize in one field of study, such as Arctic wildlife.

poaching: Illegal hunting.

predator: An animal that kills other animals for food.

prey: An animal that is hunted by a predator.

scavengers: Animals that eat prey that has been killed by other animals or that has died from other causes.

tranquilize: To put an animal to sleep for a short time with a drug. Scientists tranquilize polar bears to learn more about them and to move them to safer places. Usually, the drug is shot into the bear from a special type of gun that does not harm the animal.

trophy hunting: Hunting animals in order to display their heads, horns, or pelts.

tundra: Thick, low-growing plants that cover the ground in northern polar regions where trees cannot grow. Polar bears hunt birds and small animals that live on the tundra.

Ursus maritimus (UR-sus mare-uh-TEE-mus): The scientific name given to polar bears. In the Latin language, *ursus* means "bear," and *maritimus* means "belonging to the sea."

For Further Exploration

Books

Kelly Milner Halls, "Klondike and Snow," *Highlights for Children*, April 1997.

> In 1994 two polar bear cubs born in the Denver Zoo were abandoned by their mother. The zoo staff quickly stepped in to save them. This is the fascinating story of how a group of dedicated people successfully raised two polar bear cubs.

Thomas D. Mangelsen, *Polar Dance: Born of the North Wind*. Omaha, NE: Images of Nature, 1997.

> The brief text of this book is written for adults, but dozens of beautiful polar bear photographs make it appealing to young and old alike.

Down Matthews, *Arctic Foxes*. New York: Simon and Schuster, 1989.

> In winter, beautiful white foxes follow polar bears around to feed off prey caught by the bears. The text, written especially for young readers, is accompanied by outstanding photographs by Dan Guravich.

———, *Polar Bear Cubs*. New York: Simon and Schuster, 1995.

> This book is filled with appealing photographs of polar bear cubs taken by Arctic photographer Dan Guravich. Written for the middle grades, the text is interesting and easy to read.

Nikita Ovsyanikov, *Polar Bears: Living with the White Bear*. Stillwater, MN: Voyageur, 1996.

> The author is a Russian naturalist who studied polar bears on Wrangel Island for eight seasons (1990–1998). Children will enjoy hearing how he lived safely among polar bears without carrying a gun. The text is written for adults but the photographs are for all ages.

Sandra Chisholm Robinson, *The Everywhere Bear*. Boulder, CO: Roberts Rinehart, 1992.

> Part of the Wonder series of the Denver Museum of Natural History, this workbook contains stories, games, and activities about all kinds of bears. It is suitable for middle- and upper-elementary grades.

Kennan Ward, "Lost and All Alone," *National Geographic World*, January 1998.

> The story of how wildlife photographer Ward rescued an abandoned polar bear cub while he and his film company were working on Wrangel Island.

Websites

National Marine Mammal Laboratory Education Web Site. http://nmml01.afsc.noaa. gov/education/default.htm.

> This site is designed especially for young people. It provides reliable scientific information about all sea mammals, including seals, walruses, whales, and polar bears. It also lists books and other Internet sources for more information.

Polar Bear Web Fan Club. www.polarbear.org.uk.

> This is a very entertaining website for anyone interested in polar bears. It has features that both young and old will enjoy, including news about polar bears, pictures, games, humor, and much more.

Videos

In the Land of the Polar Bears. Stamford, CT: Vestron Video, 1989.

> This video was filmed on Wrangel Island by Russian scientist Yuri Ledin. It is part of the NOVA *Adventures in Science* television series. In addition to polar bears, the video also contains footage of other Arctic wildlife, such as snow geese, Arctic foxes, and walruses. Although there are a few hunting scenes in it, none are prolonged or shown graphically.

Index

Picture Credits

About the Author

Freelance writer Eleanor J. Hall is an avid traveler with a particular interest in wildlife and its preservation. She has held various jobs with the National Park Service from the Florida Everglades to an Inuit community in northern Alaska. She now makes her home base in St. Louis, Missouri. Her writing credits include curriculum guides for the National Park Service, magazine articles, children's activity columns for Woodall's RV Publications, and five previous books for Lucent Books.